SCIENCE IN OUR WORLD

TIME

Contributory Author
Brian Knapp, BSc, PhD
Art Director
Duncan McCrae, BSc
Special models
Tim Fulford, MA, Head of Design and Technology,
Leighton Park School
Special photography
Graham Servante
Editorial consultants
Rita Owen and Victoria Ramsay
Illustrators
David Hardy and David Woodroffe
Science advisor
Jack Brettle, BSc, PhD, Chief Research Scientist,
Pilkington plc
Print consultants
Landmark Production Consultants Ltd
Printed and bound in Hong Kong
Produced by
EARTHSCAPE EDITIONS

First published in the United Kingdom in 1992
by Atlantic Europe Publishing Company Limited,
86 Peppard Road, Sonning Common, Reading,
Berkshire, RG4 9RP, UK

Copyright © 1992
Atlantic Europe Publishing Company Limited

Publication Data

Knapp, Brian
　Time – (Science in our world; 16)
　1. Time – For children
　I. Title　　　II. Series
529.7

ISBN 1-869860-56-X

In this book you will find some words that have been shown in **bold** type. There is a full explanation of each of these words on pages 46 and 47.

On many pages you will find experiments that you might like to try for yourself. They have been put in a yellow box like this.

Acknowledgements
The publishers would like to thank the following:
Oxford University Museum, Redlands County
Primary School and Dr Richard Crocket.

Picture credits
t=top b=bottom l=left r=right

All photographs from the Earthscape Editions
photographic library except the following:
NASA 38b, 39t; ZEFA 44/45.

Contents

Introduction

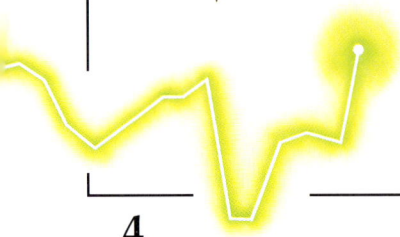

Place your hand on your chest and feel the rhythmic beating of your heart. Look at a clock's **pendulum** and hear the time tick by.

Time is a vital part of the way the Universe works. Scientists think of time as a measurable **dimension**, just like length.

In the past people could not measure time easily and they did not have the same 'sense' of time that we do today. Yet even the earliest traces of civilisations showed that people were very interested in time. The great stone slabs of England's Stonehenge, assembled over 3000 years ago, were most likely designed to show the special time of the year called midsummer's day.

The first mechanical clocks, using gear wheels, were developed 600 years ago. They were made more accurate by the discovery that a pendulum always swings in a precise, rhythmic way. In this century

people have been able to use the rhythmic movements, or vibrations, of **atoms** to measure time to an accuracy of thousandths of a second a year.

As accuracy in telling time developed, lifestyles changed. For example, in the past the working day roughly matched the length for which there was daylight to see by; now for many people it is measured to the minute by timetables, attendance cards at work and the like. For this reason some people now feel that we have become 'prisoners' of time.

But time does not just measure the passing seconds, minutes and hours for work; it can also be used to tell us, for example, where we are on Earth and how far things are apart from each other. In this book you can discover a universe of time in any way you choose. Just turn to a page and begin your discoveries.

Clocks that drive our lives

Our bodies have many natural types of 'clocks' that measure out time. For example, your pulse is a measure of the time between your heart beats; an internal 'clock' also helps you to wake up in the morning and go to sleep at night.

9.00
Breakfast

The circadian rhythm

Our pattern of sleeping and waking seems to follow a pattern which is repeated each day, that is every 24 hours. This is called the circadian rhythm and it is one of the most important uses of time in our lives.

Scientists have discovered that the timing of the circadian rhythm depends on the amount of daylight and darkness. When people have been kept in totally artificial conditions for a long time (such as in a long submarine journey), they gradually slip out of a 24-hour cycle and move into one that is 25 hours long, close to the length of the **lunar** day.

11.00
Working

Jet Lag

This is the feeling of illness people get when their own internal clock gets out of step with what is going on around them, usually as the result of a long plane journey.

Say, for example, a person flies from New York to San Francisco. Local times are three hours different, so a person flying from New York at breakfast time will arrive at breakfast time in San Francisco, but it is their internal body clock tells them its time for lunch. They are also likely to suffer poor sleep.

It can take about two days for body clocks to get in step with local time after such a journey.

19.30
Eating

Pulse time

To time your pulse, put your fingers on the inside of your wrist until you can feel the blood being pushed along your arteries. Each beat of the heart sends a new pulse of blood through the arteries and old, used blood is pushed back to the heart through the veins.

Use a stopwatch to find out how many beats you have to a second.

23.00
Sleeping

Check your body temperature

Many of your body functions are related to the time of day. To see how your body temperature changes throughout the day, for example, make a record of your temperature using a clinical thermometer (the sort that goes under your tongue). Take measurements at hourly intervals starting immediately you wake up.

The next day get someone to wake you up really early (e.g. before dawn) and again measure your temperature. Using all these measurements make a chart of the daily change in your body temperature beginning at 9 am. Does it look like the blood pressure line which has been drawn across this page?

Eating and drinking

Have you noticed how you become hungry at certain times of the day? The regular need for food is not related to the amount of work you do nor the food energy you use up, but to your circadian rhythm.

The effect of the body clock means that people who do little exercise are more likely to become overweight because they still want to eat regularly, even though their body does not need the food for energy.

The line drawn across the page represents the changes in blood pressure that occurred during a 24 hour day, beginning at 9 am.

The seasons: nature's clocks

The change in temperature, warmth and day length affect the **biological clocks** of many living things. In plants growth, flowering, fruiting and leaf fall are all connected to a yearly cycle. Many animals also have seasonal clocks.

The seasonal cycle in plants

Many plants show very marked seasonal changes which seem to be connected to some kind of internal clock. These changes appear to be triggered by some external event such as a change in day length, soil temperature or the onset of a drought.

For example, plants that live for more than one year (i.e. perennials), have cycles for growing and for shedding their leaves. In a climate with warm and cold seasons, the first signs of frosts in the autumn, for example, is often the signal for the start of leaf fall. However, even in regions with high temperatures throughout the year, trees have periods when they grow, flower, fruit and shed their leaves.

Seasonal squirrels

Squirrels are a good example of creatures that have a seasonal clock rather like an internal alarm clock. As the seasons change the 'alarm' goes off and there is a complete change in behaviour.

The squirrel gains weight in the summer and the autumn, it then **hibernates** during winter, and wakes up in spring to begin breeding.

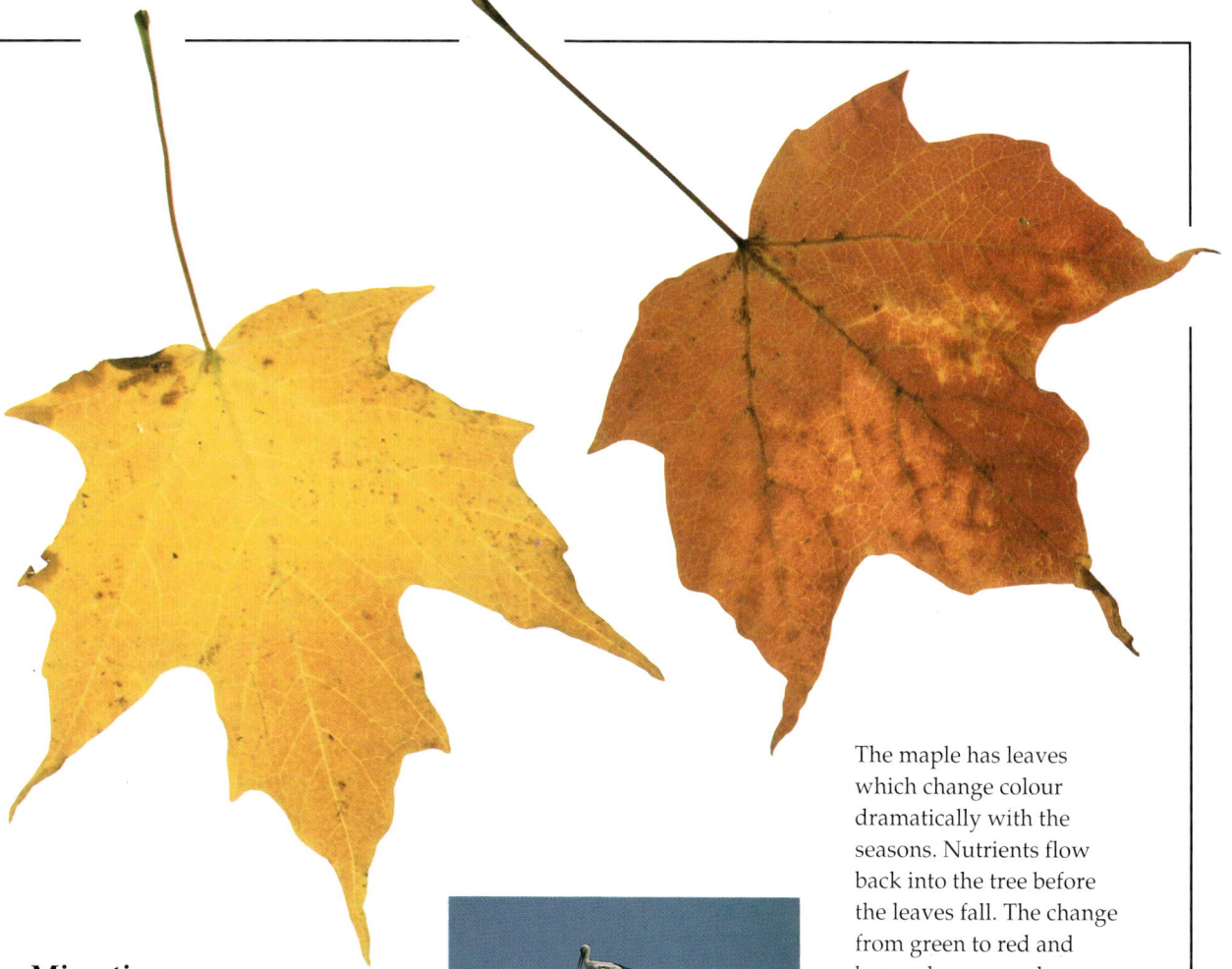

The maple has leaves which change colour dramatically with the seasons. Nutrients flow back into the tree before the leaves fall. The change from green to red and brown happens when a biological clock tells the small green pigment **chlorophyll** cells to die

Migration

Many animals **migrate** long distances at set times of the year. It is common to see, for example, huge flocks of martins or swallows wheeling in the sky before they migrate to their winter feeding grounds.

Yet although the migrations make sure that the animals move to places where they can find a winter food supply, they do not migrate when food has become short. Rather, they migrate *before* food shortages set in, showing that they are migrating because of their internal biological clocks.

Storks are typical of birds that migrate thousands of kilometres each year

Calendars

A calendar is a system for dividing the year into smaller units according to a set of rules based on the way the Earth, Sun and Moon move relative to each other.

The problem of making a calendar with equal divisions is that the Earth takes 365.2422 days to **orbit** the Sun and the Moon 29.53 days to orbit the Earth. This has meant that our calendars – which use whole numbers of days – need special rules for keeping in step.

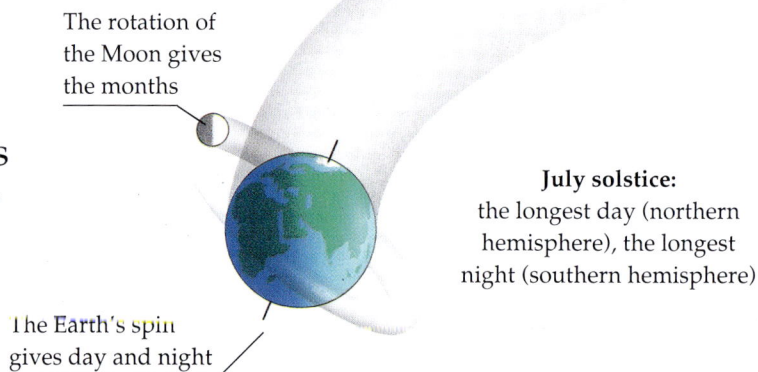

The rotation of the Moon gives the months

The Earth's spin gives day and night

The first calendars
The first calendars go back over 4000 years when stone circles were arranged to allow ancient peoples to keep track of the year. They used the position of the Sun or the Moon as it crossed the horizon.

July solstice: the longest day (northern hemisphere), the longest night (southern hemisphere)

The basis of calendars
The Earth spins on an axis making a complete turn every 24 hours which is why we experience night followed by day.

At the same time the Earth orbits the Sun. The Earth spins on a tilted **axis** (as you can see in the diagram) and this means that the height of the Sun at noon each day changes through the year. The Sun rises to its lowest noonday point in midwinter (the winter **solstice**), and it reaches its highest noonday point on midsummer's day (the summer solstice).

The Moon orbits around the Earth about once every 30 days, the length of the (**lunar**) month.

The first day
The Babylonians first began to measure time accurately using sundials. They divided the unit of time called the year, which they made 360 days long, while each month was made 30 days, giving 12 months in the year.

To improve the accuracy of the calendar, the Egyptians added five extra days to the Babylonian year and used them for feasting the arrival of the River Nile flood.

Days in the month
Ancient calendars were based on the **phases** of the Moon each night (a lunar calendar) so that the first night a new moon rose over the horizon was taken as the first of the month.

New moons are separated by 29.53 days, hence months used to have either 29 or 30 days.

When calendars changed to a year based on the rate the Earth went round the Sun (a solar year), some months had to be lengthened to make a total of 365 days.

March equinox:
equal day and night

The rotation of the Earth about the Sun gives the years

Axis

January solstice:
the longest night (northern hemisphere), the longest day (southern hemisphere)

September equinox
equal day and night

The Julian and Gregorian Calendars
The Julian Calendar was invented by Roman scientists. It was based on calculations of the way the Earth revolved around the Sun. For this reason a calendar can be calculated in advance for any year. However, the calculations proved to be not quite right and so in 1582 a modified calendar, adding leap years, was introduced by advisors to Pope Gregory XIII.

The Gregorian calendar is the one in use today.

Tree ring timekeepers

Many plants and animals keep an accurate record, or calendar, of the way they have grown. Trees, for example, add an extra ring of growth each year. This can be clearly seen in any cross-section of a branch or trunk.

Climate timekeepers

Tree rings tell us much about a region's past **climate**. For example, a wide ring forms when the weather is mild and rainfall is plentiful. A narrow ring hints of drought or cold, and a cracked ring tells of an ancient fire.

By counting the annual rings we can make a climate calendar that can stretch back thousands of years.

Through the use of tree rings people have discovered that there have been several very cold periods in the recent past. Changes in the width of tree rings is also helpful in showing that the Earth is warming due to the **Greenhouse Effect**.

Only saw dead wood of fallen trees for this investigation. Do not harm living trees. Be careful with sharp saws.

Count the years on a tree

Use a hand lens to examine the rings on the oak trunk shown on this page. Find out how old it is and when there were warm, moist years and when they were cool or dry.

There will also be many dead and fallen branches in a forest that you can examine. With the help of an adult, saw a section of a thick branch so that you can see the rings. Count the rings to find out how old the branch was before it fell, then look at each ring to tell what the past weather changes have been.

The oldest living timekeeper

In the western mountains of North America the Bristlecone pine grows very slowly. Scientists have found out how old these trees are by taking minute core samples from their trunks.

The oldest Bristlecone pine so far measured began life as a seed over 4900 years ago. Each ring helps to give a picture of the climate over this long period of time.

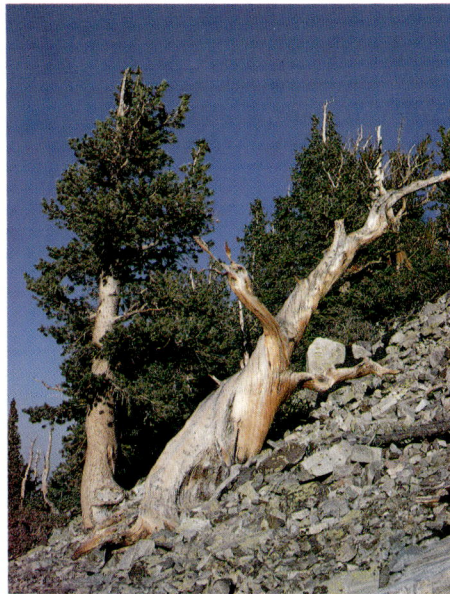

The home of Bristlecone pines is in the cold, high mountains of the western USA

There are 97 rings on this cross section of a tree trunk

Lifespans

One generation

Joanne (female)
born 1837, died 1898

married Remmel (male)
born 1832, died 1870

9 children

of whom

150 years ago

Martin (male)
born 1859, died 1928

married Virginia (female)
born 1852, died 1914

6 children

of whom

Sara Jane (female)
born 1878, died 1952

married John (male)
born 1880, died 1943

7 children

of whom

Ronald (male)
born 1899, died 1978

100 years ago

married Rose (female)
born 1903

5 children

of whom

Margaret (female)
born 1925

married Nicholas (male)
born 1930

2 children

of whom

50 years ago

Anne (female)
born 1958

married Marek (male)
born 1955

2 children

Today   **Gillian** (female)
born 1984

Leona (female)
born 1986

Each of us has a certain length of time to live. It is called our lifespan. For many people in the world's wealthier, or developed, countries the expected lifespan is over 70 years; for those in poorer, or developing, countries it may be as little as 40 years.

Child-bearing usually happens when women are between 15 and 35 and most children in developed countries are, on average, 23 years younger than their parents (18 years in the developing world). It means that about every two decades there is a new generation in a family. Lifespans and generations are therefore rough, but important, measures of time.

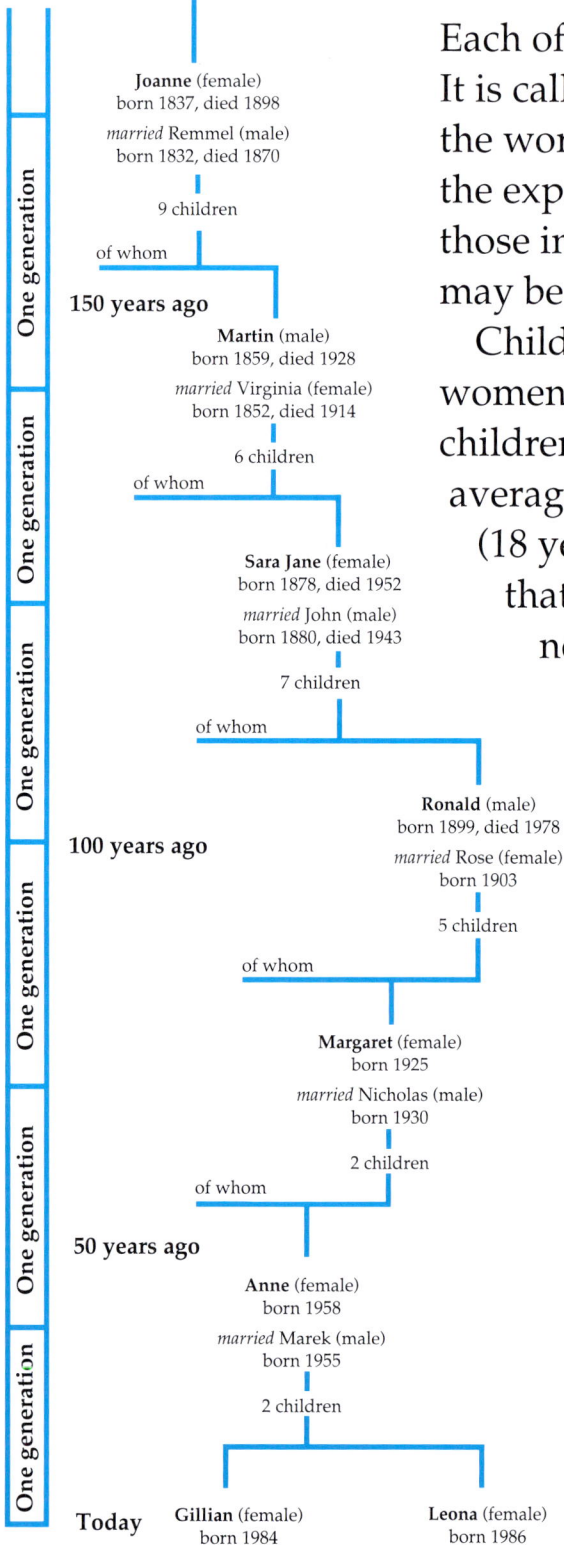

Family tree
A family tree is a way of looking back over your family in time. It traces the history of your relatives.

Try to find out about your own family tree by asking your older relatives to describe as many members of the family as they can think of. You can then make a chart of the family tree similar to the one shown on the left.

There are official records about your family kept by government offices, and with the help of an older relative, you may be able to visit a record office and trace your family tree back for centuries. (The Church of the Latter Day Saints (Mormons) have specialised in keeping family records and they have gathered them from all over the world.)

14

Place your food sample in a closed container

Moulds

Find out about mould generations. Put a piece of bread into a dish. Each day take a photograph (perhaps with an instant camera). Remember, it is important that the bread is kept moist and at a constant temperature. How many days does it take for the area of mould on the bread to double?

Population explosions

In general terms, the smaller the creature, the shorter its lifespan and the less time there is between generations. **Microscopic** organisms, such as bacteria and some fungi (that make moulds), produce new generations quickly. Bacteria, for example, produce a new generation every twenty minutes. This means that, while a single new generation of people have been born, over 625,000 generations of bacteria will have been born.

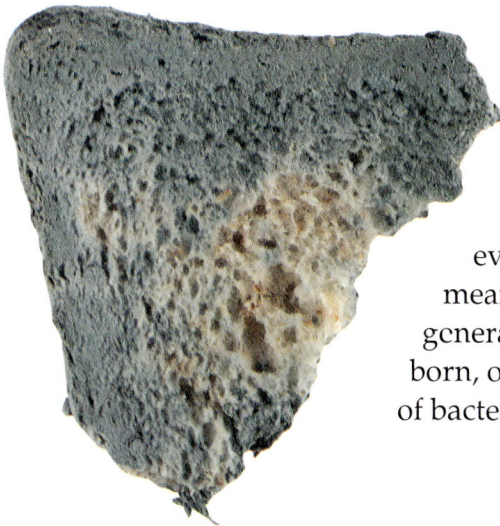

Changes with time

Imagine that some of the individual bacteria in each generation are just slightly different from the generation before them. Over the time it takes for a single human generation there will have been time for 625,000 sets of changes in the bacteria.

Because bacteria multiply so rapidly there is a good chance that many **mutations** will occur. This explains, for example, why some disease-producing organisms will often quickly become resistant to a particular medicine.

15

Old timekeepers

Time seems an easy thing to measure. It is simply a matter of looking at a clock. But it was very difficult for the first scientists to devise a way of measuring time, and very few 'timekeepers' were accurate or looked like the clocks we are used to seeing today.

Candle and oil-burning clocks

A candle will burn evenly if it is kept away from draughts and it can be marked off in bands to show the hours at night.

An oil-burning clock is an oil lamp with a glass reservoir. As the oil is burned, the oil level in the reservoir falls. A scale etched on to the reservoir tells how many hours have passed.

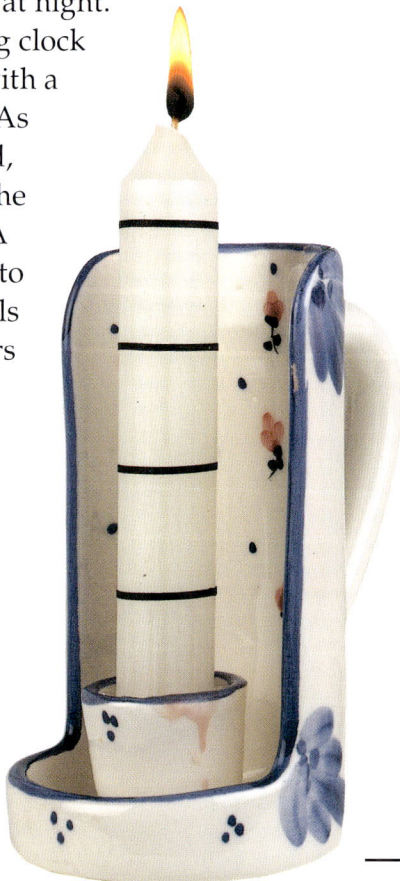

An hour glass

This is a device for measuring short periods of time, such as an hour. Sand flows from one glass bulb to the other through a narrow joining hole.

When the sand has run through, the glass is turned over and a new hour is counted.

Flowing sand in a small glass is sometimes used for timing eggs in kitchens even today.

Water -clock

To tell short intervals of time it used to be common to make a water clock by filling an earthenware bowl with water. Near the bottom of the bowl was a small hole that let water drip out.

You can make a water-clock using a set of plastic containers. You will have to experiment with the size of hole.

Use a watch to time the flow of water out of the container and make marks on the side of the container to indicate one minute and five minutes. Can you make one that will last for eight hours?

Make a clepsydra

The clepsydra is an especially refined kind of water-clock that was invented by the Egyptians 3000 years ago. It is easy to make one using some plastic tube attached to a water supply, a tube clamp or tap and a small float.

As water drips from the tube it fills the cylinder at a constant rate. This causes the float to move higher and makes the wire pointer move across the scale.

Make up the model as shown in the picture, then arrange for the water to drip out very slowly, about five drops a minute. Try to think of ways of providing a portable water supply for the tube.

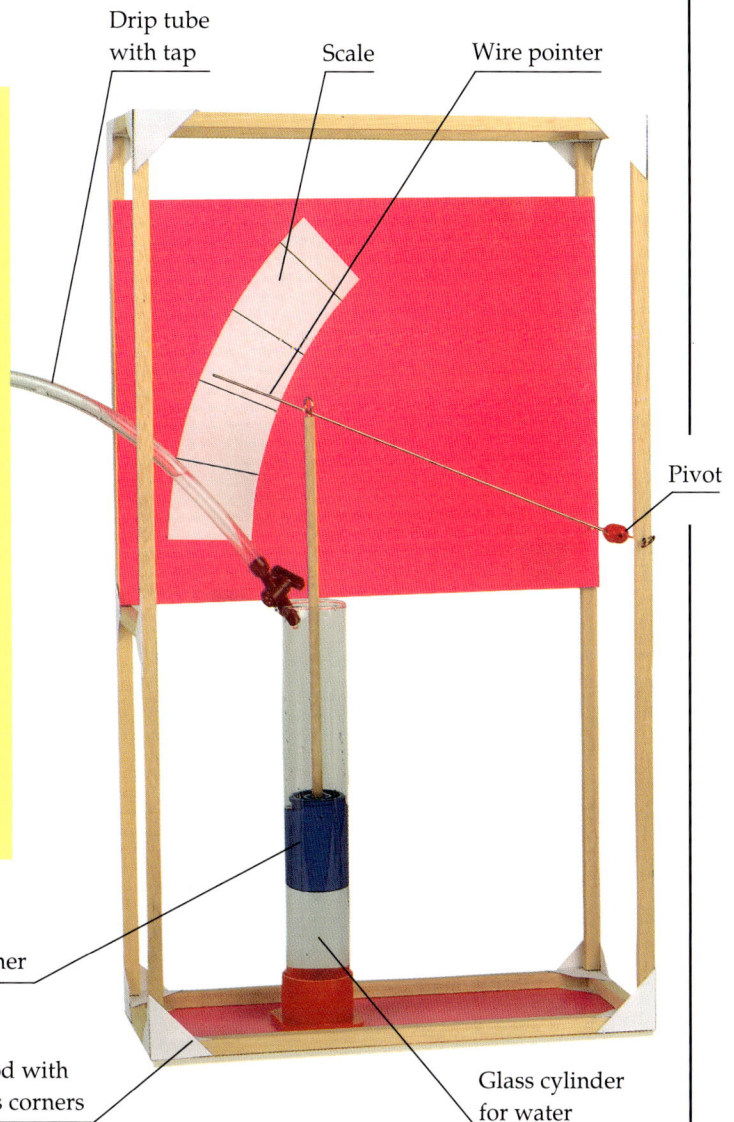

Drip tube with tap

Scale

Wire pointer

Pivot

Float made from sealed plastic container

The frame is made from wood with paper triangles pasted across corners

Glass cylinder for water

Finding the time of day

Although very simple clocks give a rough estimate of time, people have always wanted to have something which was more accurate.

Even 3600 years ago the Egyptians had refined the science of **astronomy** to give more accurate measures of time, but it was the needs of monks that led to modern clocks and timekeeping.

a.m. and p. m.
a.m. (or am) is shortened Latin for *ante meridiem* (before the meridian, the time when the Sun is highest in the sky) and p.m. (or pm) means *post* (after) *meridiem*.

This sun-dial is on the face of a memorial. A mechanical clock has also been fitted to the tower (they read one hour different because of daylight savings time)

Shadow-clock
You can make a shadow- clock by placing an upright stick on the ground. Place a stone where the shadow falls each hour.

Sun-dials and shadow-clocks
The Babylonians, 3000 years ago, were the first people known to have used shadow-clocks to measure time.

A more accurate form of shadow-clock is a sun-dial. A sun-dial was the most common means of measuring time until the mechanical clock was invented just over 600 years ago.

Month

Hour

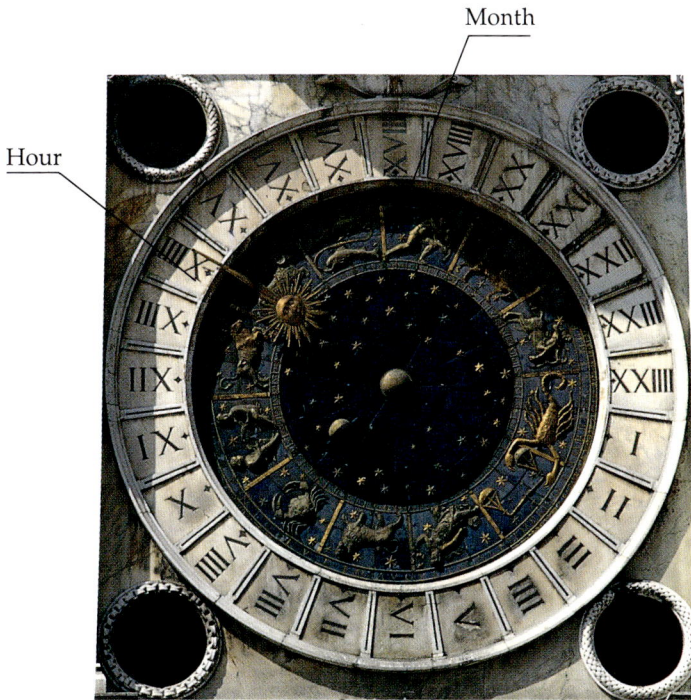

Bell rings as
the statues turn

Grand clocks such as the one in St Mark's Square, Venice,
Italy, seen above, were designed to tell many things about
the time. However, they could only be made really
accurate after the invention of the pendulum (see page 20)

The monks needed . . .

Medieval monks thought it was vital to
have accurate timekeeping for their
daily acts of worship.

By the thirteenth century a mechanical
clock had been invented that rang bells
to summon monks to prayer. It was
designed to be heard rather than seen
and it did not have a dial.

The modern word clock comes from
the French word for bell – *cloche*.

Although the monks were first to use bells for
telling the time, many public clocks were built
with bells to make it easier for the general public
to know the time of day even if they were not in
sight of the clock. Some were given added
interest by the use of moving statues

The pendulum

The properties of a pendulum – a weight swinging from a fixed point – were among the most important discoveries in time measurement.

When it is swinging across a small **arc**, a pendulum takes the same amount of time to complete its swing, no matter how much of a push it is given and no matter how heavy the weight on the end.

The discovery of this natural timekeeper soon revolutionised timekeeping.

Galileo discovered . . .
The pendulum was first introduced to European science by Galileo in the sixteenth century. One day he was sitting in the cathedral in Pisa, Italy, and he noticed an incense burner swinging to and fro. By using his pulse as a timekeeper he was able to discover that the time (called the **period**) of the swing does not change even when the size of the swing changes.

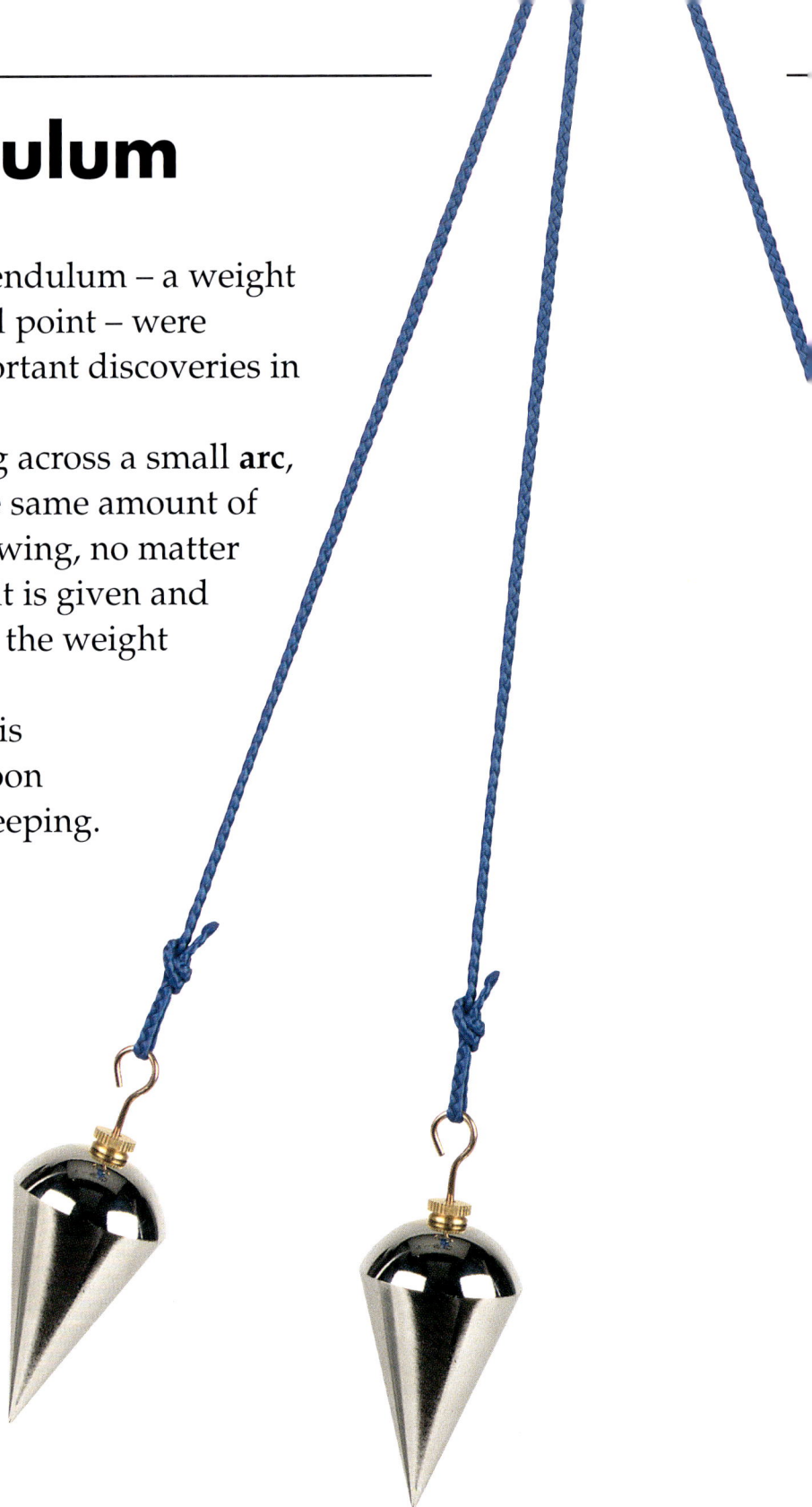

Find out about a pendulum

You can investigate the way a pendulum works using a small weight and a string.

Fix the string over a hook so the weight can swing freely. Now measure and record the length of the string. Give the weight a small push so that the swing is always quite small (less than 10 degrees). Use a stopwatch to count the time it takes for ten complete swings.

Add an extra weight without changing the length of the string and count ten swings again. Compare the result with your first measurement.

Now double the length of the string and repeat the experiment. Does changing length or adding weights affect the time period of the swing? Does the period change as the swing gets smaller?

A metronome is used for keeping time in music. It consists of a rod (the pendulum) that swings to and fro on a pivot hidden inside a box. The small weight on the exposed part of the pendulum is used to control the speed of the swing

Clocks with pendulums

The key to all clocks is to find a way of moving the hands at an even speed. For centuries a pendulum controlled the turning of gear wheels attached to the hands. Here is the principle on which such clocks were based.

The bar controls the release of each tooth

Pivot

This rocking bar is the escapement

This toothed wheel is being driven by a falling weight. In a clock the spindle carrying the toothed wheel is attached to other gear wheels which turn the clock hands

An escapement

A pendulum (or its portable equivalent called a hair spring, see page 24) is linked to a clock through a controlling mechanism called an escapement.

As the pendulum swings to and fro it rocks a bar on which there are two pegs. At each rock of the bar a peg is pulled clear of the wheel, allowing the wheel to turn by one more tooth as the other peg engages. It is named an escapement because it allows the teeth on the gear to 'escape' one by one in a regular and even manner. A complete swing of the pendulum is shown in the pictures on the opposite page.

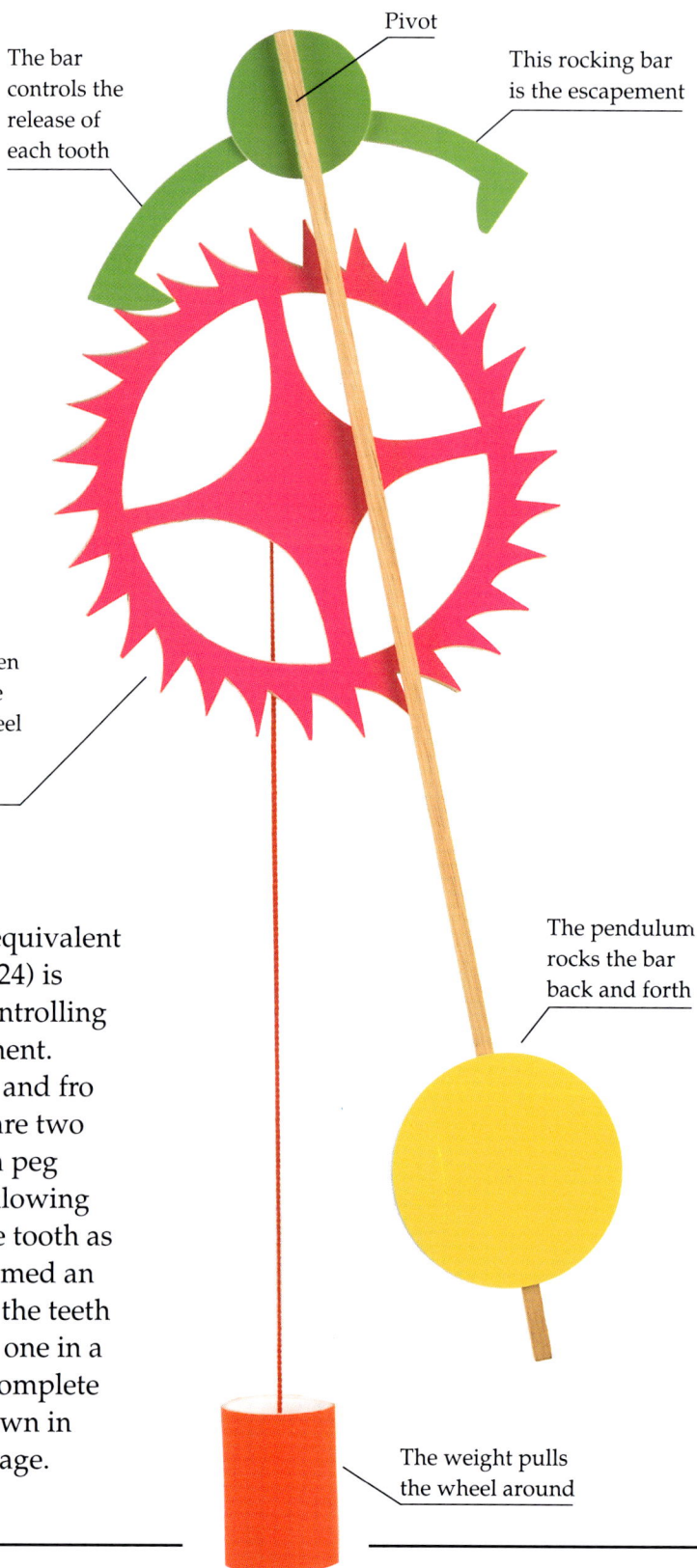

The pendulum rocks the bar back and forth

The weight pulls the wheel around

How pendulum clocks work

All mechanical clocks must have their own source of energy such as a falling weight or a spring. The clock is made accurate by controlling, or regulating, the energy source.

Falling weights or a spring turn a system of gear wheels that move the hands of the clock.

1

long arm

Short arm

Pendulum is at its farthest right. The rocking bar holds the teeth

2

Pendulum swings to the left, the rocking bar disengages and the wheel is pulled round by the weight. It moves one tooth on before it is trapped by the short arm of the rocking bar

A weight-driven clock

In a weight-driven clock the energy to turn the wheels is provided by a heavy weight. As the weight falls it tries to turn the wheels, but is controlled by an escapement.

3

Pendulum swings back to the right again, allowing the wheel to be pulled round one more tooth

Make a clock

You can make an escapement and show that the rocking pendulum controls the wheel. Make a very accurate tracing of the parts shown on the opposite page, then cut them out of stiff card or card-faced foam sheet. Once assembled you have made the basis of a clock.

Spring-driven clocks

Most of the clocks that were in use until a few years ago (when digital clocks were invented) were called **mechanical** clocks. They used a series of toothed wheels, connected together in such a way that the hour, minute and second hands were all driven from the same weight or spring.

Spring-driven clocks, and especially wrist-watches, are among the most precise mechanical things ever made.

Gears for minute hand

Hair spring

Gears for hour hand

This modern wrist-watch gives you some idea of the precision engineering that is needed to turn the principles of science into usable machines

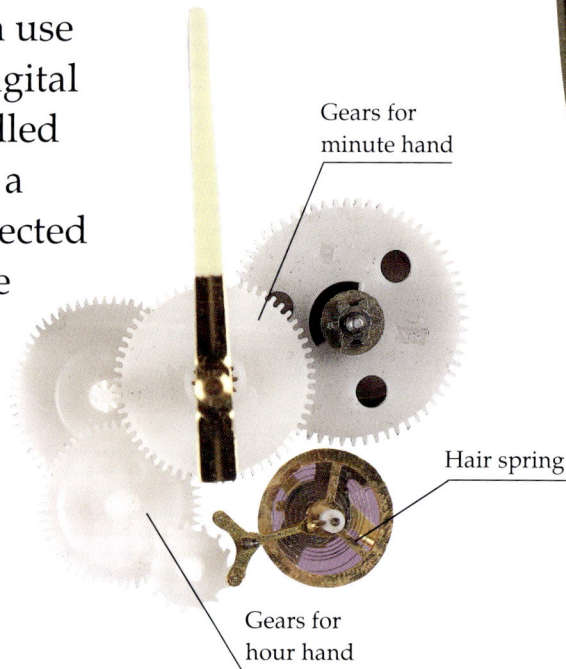

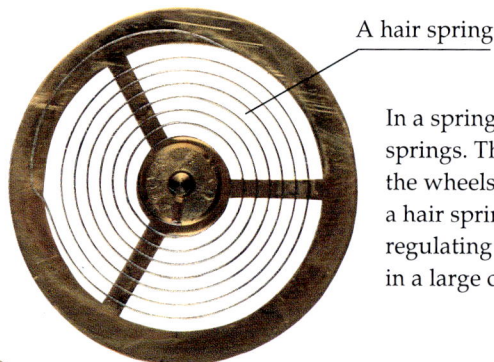

A hair spring

In a spring-driven clock there are two springs. The large main spring drives the wheels. The small spring – called a hair spring – does the same job of regulating the speed as the pendulum in a large clock as it curls and uncurls

The spindles of the wheels turn in tiny cups – called bearings – made from very hard stone such as ruby. Using hard stone makes the bearing last a long time before it wears loose. The rubies are the small pink objects. Many watches have at least seven jewels

17 JEWE

BEZEL MIYOTA JAPAN

Hairspring

Escapement

Jewelled bearing

Portable, spring-driven clocks

Weights and pendulums make clocks accurate but
they are not easy to carry around. So the spring-
driven clock was invented.

In a spring-driven clock the weight is replaced by
a coiled main spring. The main spring is attached to
a gear wheel, and as the main spring tries to uncurl it
turns the gear wheel which in turn moves the hands
round the dial. The speed of turning is controlled by
a small escapement fixed to a hair spring.

A modern mechanical watch
with a transparent case.
Notice how the mechanism
is beautifully engineered

*(For more information on the pendulum
see the volume* Falling (Gravity) *in the
Science in our World series.)*

Quartz time

Quartz is the most common **mineral** to be found on the face of the Earth. But this simple mineral has revolutionised the way we keep and use time, because it can be made to vibrate and do the same job as a pendulum. As a result it forms the 'heart' of most modern watches and clocks.

How the watch works

Just as a tuning fork struck on a table vibrates in a certain way, so a quartz crystal will vibrate when it is struck by an electrical voltage from a tiny battery.

A quartz crystal vibrates 32,768 times a second. Simple electrical circuits count the number of vibrations and when 32,768 have been recorded, they send a pulse of electricity which moves the dial on the watch face a further one second.

Because quartz vibrates at a constant rate, even cheap watches can be made accurate to within a second a day.

In the small watch on your wrist there is a computer, a tuning fork and a space-age display. Here you can see it separated out to show the main parts

Special filters placed in front and behind the crystal make the display visible

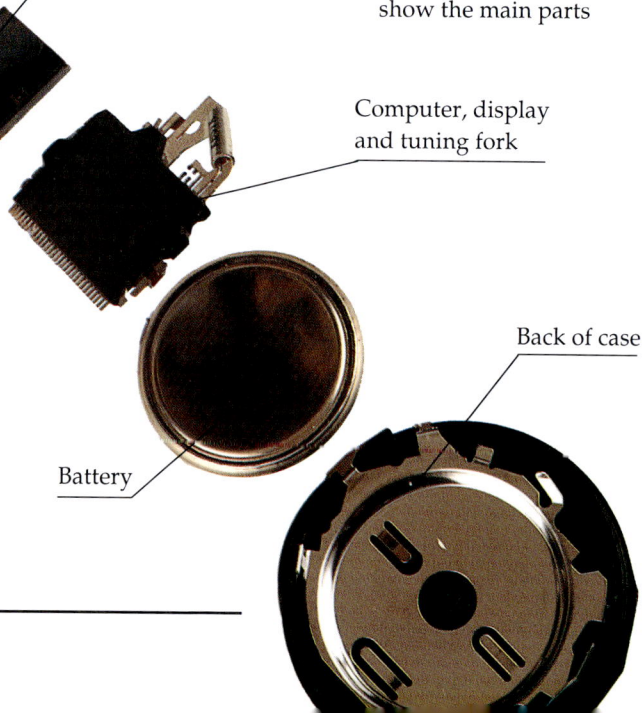

Computer, display and tuning fork

Quartz crystals

The use of the quartz crystal in watches and clocks is a very modern invention: the first watch to use a quartz crystal was made as recently as 1969. This was the year the Japanese company Seiko found out how to turn the quartz crystal into a tiny tuning fork.

Battery

Back of case

display

Face

Mass-produced time

The use of quartz crystals has enabled watches to be produced more rapidly and more cheaply than ever before. About a half billion watches are made each year, enough for everyone in the world within 20 years.

Quartz crystal tuning fork. This tuning fork is just 5 mm long yet it is vital in controlling the accuracy of a quartz watch

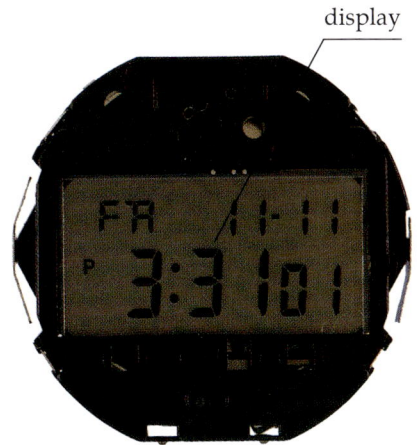

The face of a watch with a digital read-out is made of a material called a liquid crystal. The crystal switches from dark to clear on signals from the watch's internal counter. The counter can also send pulses to a tiny motor to drive a pair of hands

The battery powers the **chip** computer and keeps the crystal vibrating. This rhythmic vibration is fed back to the counter to move on the display very accurately

Back

Silicon chip computer counts the pulses

Timing and timetables

In our busy world making sure things happen on time can make life easier. For example, you may use a timetable to make sure you arrive on time or to save waiting too long for a connection.

By studying timing scientifically it is possible to 'save' time and money. Here are some examples.

Timetables

A timetable is a way of organising busy networks as efficiently as possible. Bus, airline, ferry or rail timetables are clear examples. Railways can make the best use of their track by using a timetable. For example, several trains can use a single platform if a timetable tells them when to arrive and depart.

A radio and TV guide is a timetable. All the programmes are scheduled and published in newspapers and magazines so that the viewers know when to watch the programmes of their choice.

TV and radio programmes are often arranged to make it easy for viewers to switch channels without missing the start or end of their favourite programmes

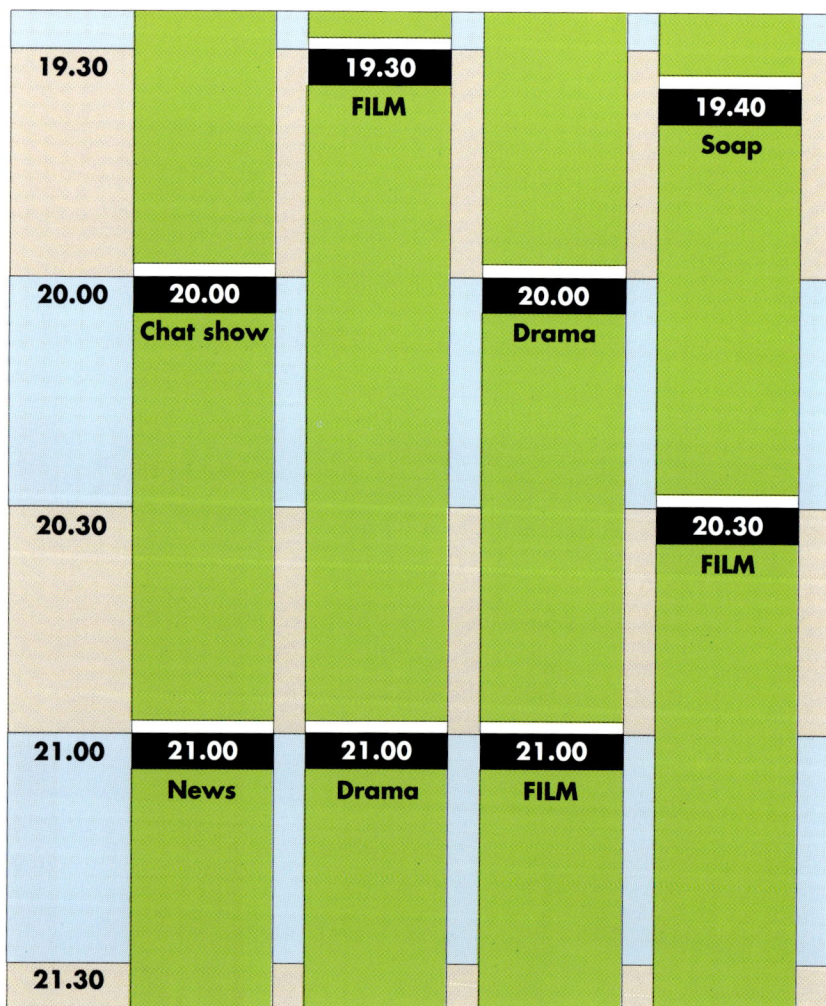

Time				
19.30		**19.30** FILM		
				19.40 Soap
20.00	**20.00** Chat show		**20.00** Drama	
20.30				**20.30** FILM
21.00	**21.00** News	**21.00** Drama	**21.00** FILM	
21.30				

28

School timetables

A school timetable is a way of dividing the day and the pupils into working groups.

Study your school's timetable and try to find out how it has been organised. You may find that the teacher responsible uses a board filled with pegs of different shapes and colours, or they might use a computer to do the job.

With some friends, begin to make up a school timetable for yourself. First try to find out what information you might need to construct the timetable, then think out how to arrange each class through the day. Is it easier if classes move between rooms or if they stay in the same room throughout the day?

Traffic lights

Traffic lights are used at busy junctions to speed up the flow of traffic. Each route in turn is given a certain length of time to clear. By carefully setting this time vehicles are moved through a busy junction with the minimum possible waiting time. If too short an interval is allowed the traffic never gets a chance to get under way and the junction always has vehicles waiting; if the time interval is too long vehicles may have to wait at a junction unnecessarily even after other routes have cleared.

Navigating with time

When sailors are on the open oceans they have no landmarks to tell them where they are. So how do they navigate from one place to another successfully? The answer is partly by using time.

A grid for the Earth

It is much easier to know where you are on Earth if the surface is divided up by sets of lines. One set of lines (called lines of latitude) are drawn running parallel to the Equator, the other set (called meridians, or lines of longitude) running through the Poles. The crossing of lines makes a grid.

To find where you are, you need to know which part of the grid you are in. Sailors can find out the latitude by using the height of the overhead Sun by day or certain stars by night. They find the longitude by using a clock set to the time at Greenwich in London, UK.

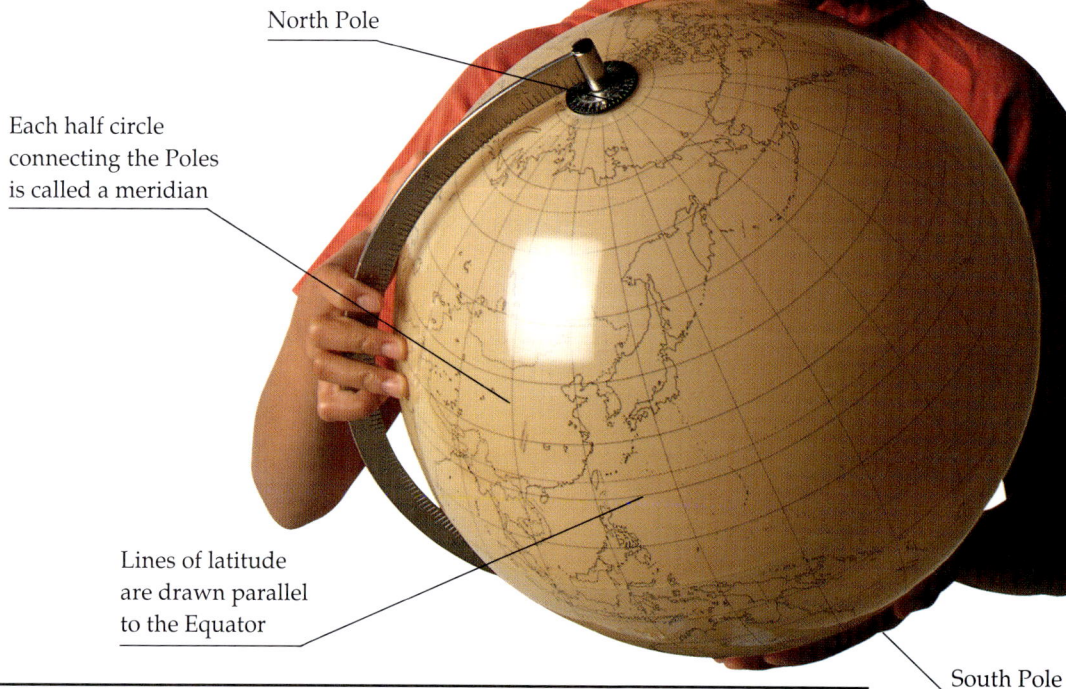

North Pole

Each half circle connecting the Poles is called a meridian

Lines of latitude are drawn parallel to the Equator

South Pole

Greenwich (London) is on the 0° longitude line. It is called the Prime Meridian

A line of longitude

A line of latitude

Greenwich Mean Time

There is no special scientific reason to choose Greenwich, UK as the place for 0 degrees longitude – called the Prime Meridian. It was done by international agreement at a meeting in Washington, USA in 1884 because the British astronomical observatory – where accurate measurements of longitude could be made – was sited at Greenwich.

All clocks used for navigation at sea are set to Greenwich Mean Time. Checks of the exact time are given on the shipping frequencies of many radio stations throughout the world. You may have recognised them as a set of 'pips'.

In the age of sail all ships navigated by accurate clocks called chronometers. Modern ships use computers to receive signals from satellites orbiting the Earth. Because they are in fixed known positions computers can calculate both latitude and longitude, day or night.

Longitude

If it is noon at Greenwich it is midnight on the opposite side of the world. This means that the world can be divided into lines which are at the same time (see Time Zones, page 32).

If you have a clock set to give the correct time at Greenwich (called Greenwich Mean Time, GMT) and you look at your clock when the Sun is at its highest in the sky (local noon), the difference in hours between the clock and noon tells you how far around the world you are from Greenwich, that is it gives you your longitude.

Time zones

Because the Earth revolves around the Sun, some places will be in darkness when others are in light, some will see the Sun setting and call their time afternoon, when others see the Sun rising and speak of morning. This means that the time in each region of the world must be adjusted to match the time when locally the Sun is overhead at midday. The way of getting over this problem is to divide up the world into bands with the same time. They are called time zones.

Time zones stretch from pole to pole because the Earth rotates around the poles

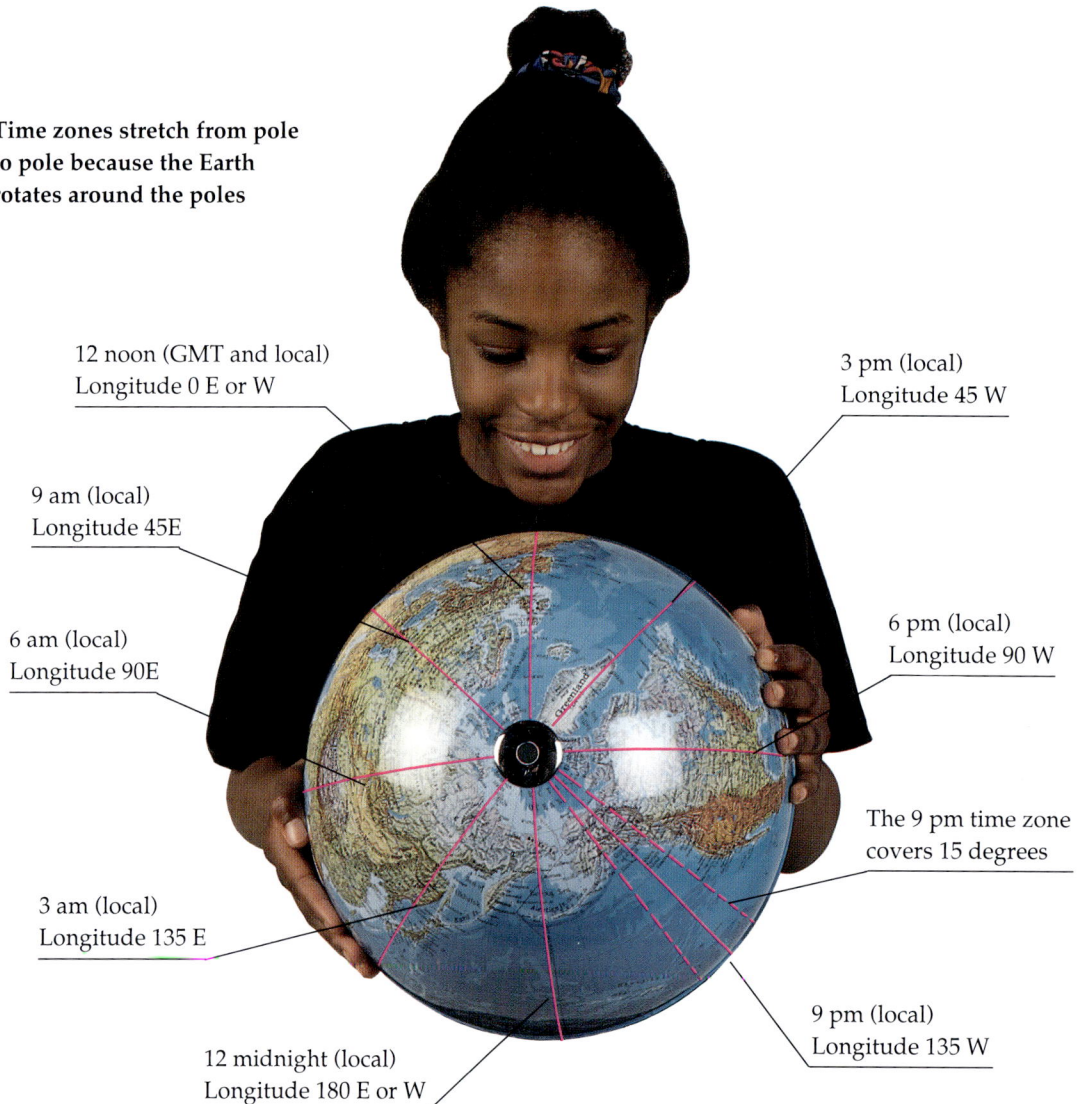

12 noon (GMT and local)
Longitude 0 E or W

3 pm (local)
Longitude 45 W

9 am (local)
Longitude 45E

6 am (local)
Longitude 90E

6 pm (local)
Longitude 90 W

The 9 pm time zone covers 15 degrees

3 am (local)
Longitude 135 E

12 midnight (local)
Longitude 180 E or W

9 pm (local)
Longitude 135 W

This picture shows Greenwich in London. The observatory is the domed building on the skyline between the towers

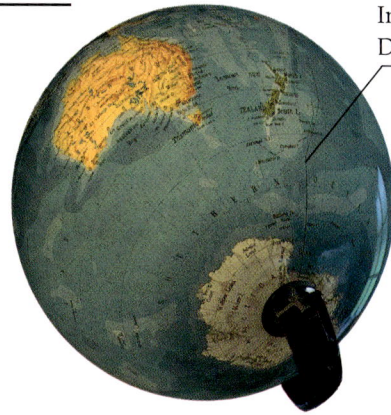

24/0 hours
International
Date Line

How time zones are set

A time zone is a longitudinal strip of the Earth's surface that stretches from pole to pole and in which everyone shares the same time of day or night. Each time zone covers 15 degrees of the globe because the Earth rotates 360 degrees once every 24 hours.

For various reasons, however, some countries choose to belong to a time zone different from their 'natural' zone.

Understand time zones

You can make your own time zone predictor by tracing out the map shown below. Do not copy the time lines. Stick the end flaps together to make a cylinder.

Trace the time lines on to a piece of tracing paper and stick the ends together to make a cylinder that slips over the map cylinder.

Put the time you choose over a city (say 8 p.m. at Adelaide, Australia) and read off from the cylinder the time elsewhere (for example, it will be 2 a.m. in Vancouver, Canada and 10 a.m. in London, UK).

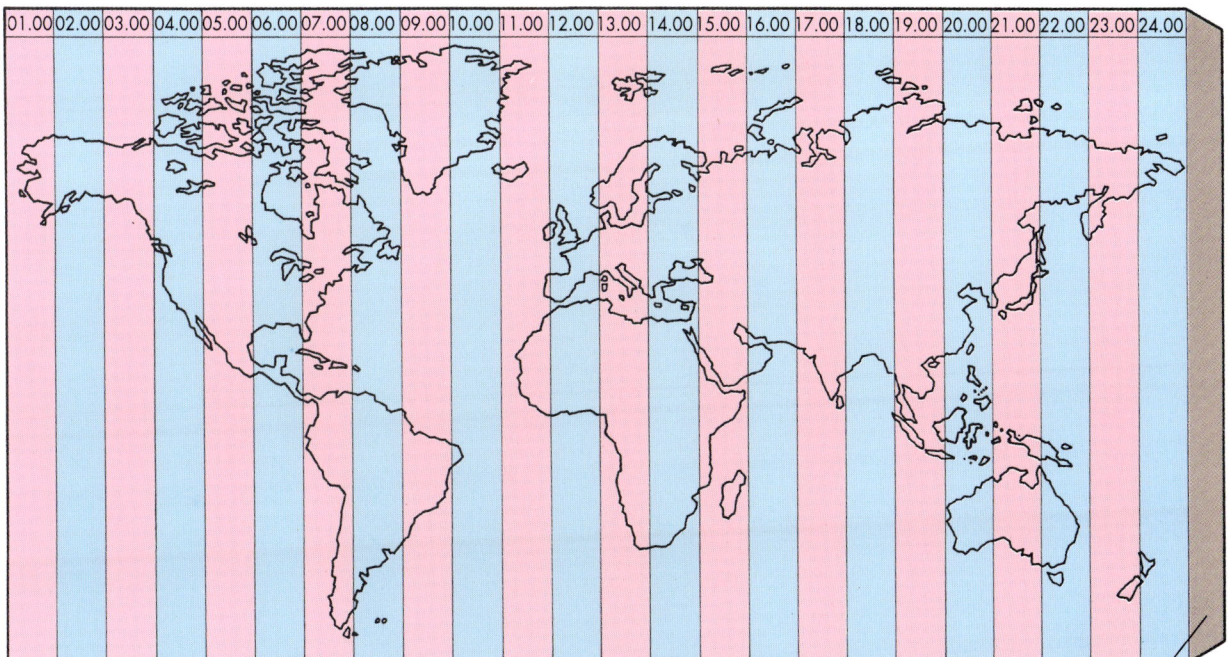

| 01.00 | 02.00 | 03.00 | 04.00 | 05.00 | 06.00 | 07.00 | 08.00 | 09.00 | 10.00 | 11.00 | 12.00 | 13.00 | 14.00 | 15.00 | 16.00 | 17.00 | 18.00 | 19.00 | 20.00 | 21.00 | 22.00 | 23.00 | 24.00 |

Flap

Measuring time with atoms

Atoms are the incredibly tiny building blocks of everything in the Universe, from the largest star to the air we breathe.

Atoms are phenomenally accurate timekeepers, so the way to measure time very precisely is to measure the way atoms behave.

The age of this fossilised tree trunk can be measured by using potassium dating. This tells us how long ago the tree lived

Uranium time

Uranium is a radioactive metal that is found quite commonly in rocks. Because uranium is radioactive it gives out energy all the time at a known slow rate. Rocks that are hundreds of millions of years old still show some radioactivity and therefore scientists can use this property as a measure of time. Uranium is one of several **elements** used by geologists to measure the age of very old rocks. Others include potassium and rubidium.

The atomic clock

There are many elements that are suitable for use in atomic clocks. The most commonly used is called cesium, but it is also possible to use hydrogen, which is one of the substances that makes water. It takes very special equipment to make an atomic clock, and it is far too expensive for general use. For this reason only a few atomic clocks have been built. All other clocks are set by them, including the 'pips' sent out over the radio to mark the time.

The accuracy given by an atomic clock is to within one second in 30,000 years.

This is a piece of coal which has been dated at 330 million years old

Carbon time

Inside virtually every living thing there is an atomic clock, the carbon clock. Our bodies and the tissues of plants, are all made of a substance called carbon – which also makes coal.

There is a special type of carbon that is formed in the air and which can only be absorbed as living things breathe. It is called carbon 14. It gives out tiny amounts of radioactivity that can only be detected using special scientific instruments.

When a living thing dies it stops absorbing this special form of carbon and the radioactivity gradually gets weaker and weaker - a process called radioactive decay. Scientists can measure how weak the radiation has become in dead tissues and from this they can tell the age of many things, such as buried bodies, mummies in tombs and trees buried in peat bogs.

The age of this mammoth's tooth can be measured by carbon 14 dating. This tells us how long ago the mammoth lived

The age of the *wood* used for this wrecked sailing ship can be measured by radio-carbon dating. But it *cannot* measure the date of the shipwreck

The geological record of time

Over many millions of years, one group of interbreeding creatures (a species) may change, or **evolve**, so much that its shape is clearly different from its ancestors.

Since life first began on Earth there have been numerous evolutionary changes, and from them scientists have been able to make a time scale called the geological record.

The use of geological time
Geological time spreads out important events that occurred during the Earth's history more evenly than if real time were used, but the disadvantage is that geological periods do not cover equal lengths of time.

A trilobite

570 million years ago

500 million years ago

430 million years ago

395 million years ago

345 million years ago

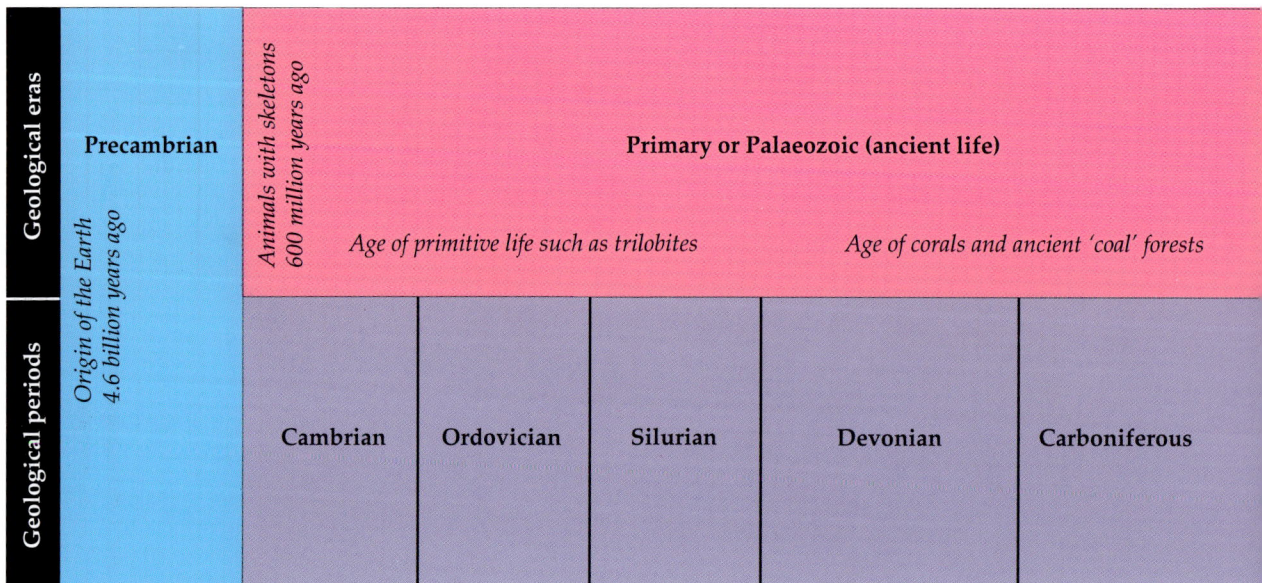

Geological eras	Precambrian	Primary or Palaeozoic (ancient life)				
	Origin of the Earth 4.6 billion years ago	*Animals with skeletons 600 million years ago*	*Age of primitive life such as trilobites*		*Age of corals and ancient 'coal' forests*	
Geological periods		Cambrian	Ordovician	Silurian	Devonian	Carboniferous

Marking geological time

When geologists first studied the age of rocks they had no means of measuring the real date at which each rock had been formed. So they used **fossils** found in the rocks as an indicator of geologic time. For convenience time was worked out on the basis of major changes in fossil record. For example, from time to time many creatures on Earth became extinct and completely new ones took their place. Each long period between major changes was called a geological period and given a name (e.g. Carboniferous, meaning period of the coal forests).

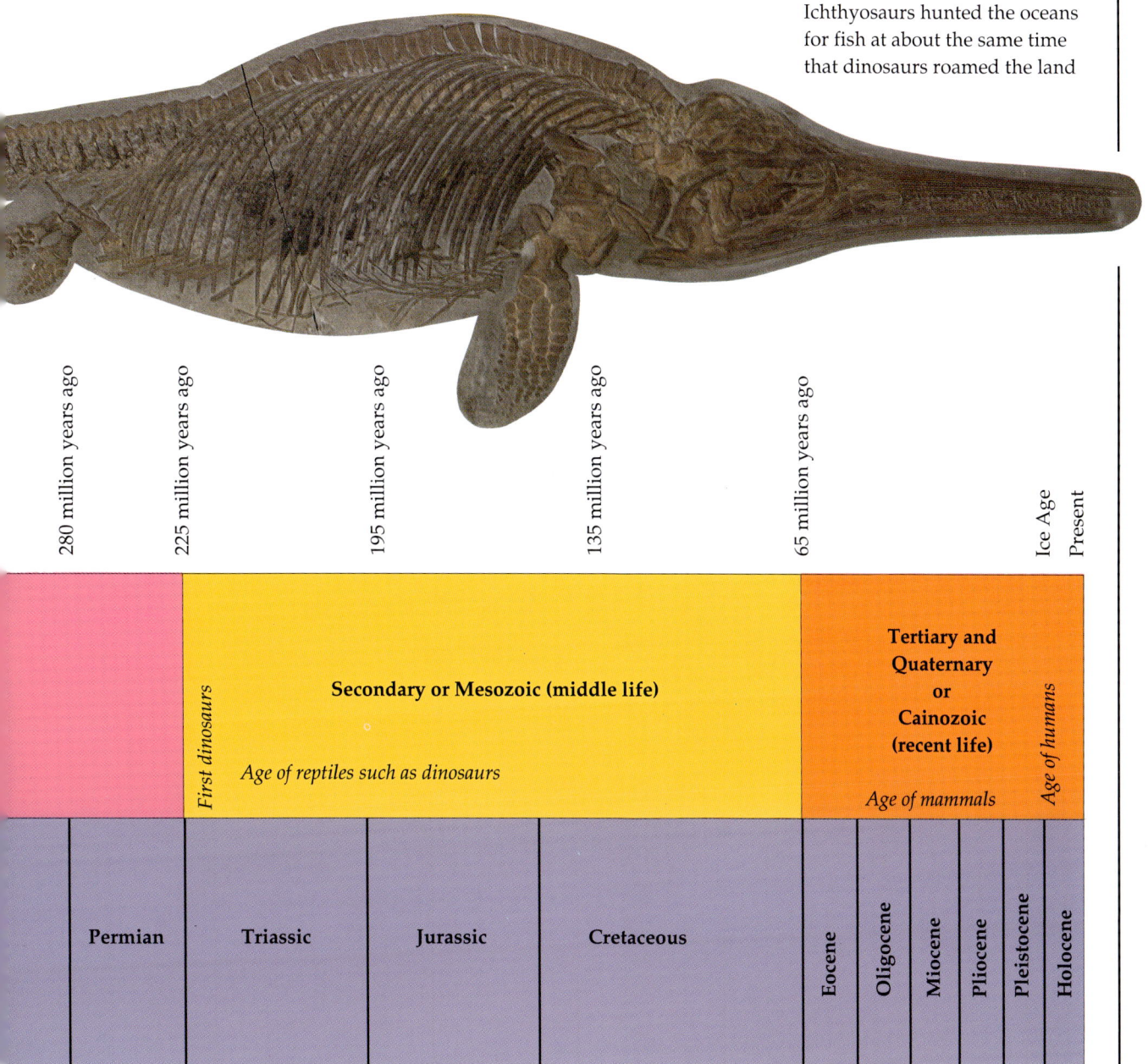

Ichthyosaurs hunted the oceans for fish at about the same time that dinosaurs roamed the land

280 million years ago	225 million years ago	195 million years ago	135 million years ago	65 million years ago	Ice Age / Present

	First dinosaurs — Secondary or Mesozoic (middle life) / Age of reptiles such as dinosaurs			Tertiary and Quaternary or Cainozoic (recent life) / Age of mammals	Age of humans
Permian	Triassic	Jurassic	Cretaceous	Eocene	Oligocene	Miocene	Pliocene	Pleistocene	Holocene

Distance and time

Imagine switching on a flashlight for a moment and then counting the seconds as the beam of light travels to the Moon, bounces from its surface and then speeds back to Earth again.

Then imagine using the time to work out how far the Moon is from the Earth. An unlikely story? In fact that is just what a laser can do.

The way we use light for time
All light travels at about 300,000 km per second. This means that the time it takes for light to travel can be used to measure distance.

The Moon is 400,000 km from the Earth, so light travels to the Moon and back in just under three seconds.

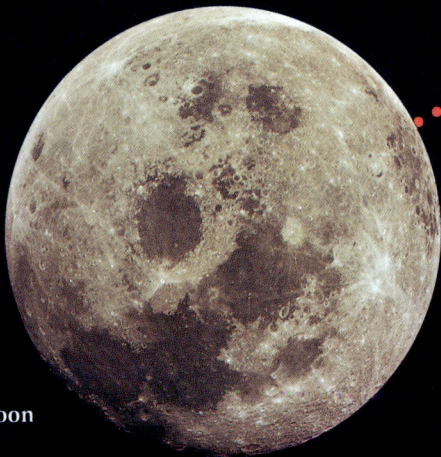

Moon

What a laser does
A laser is a machine for making rapid flashes of light. The flashes are very precise and very short, and they can be made into a very narrow beam.

A laser beam can be made so narrow that a flash of light can be bounced off the Moon and back to a receiver on Earth.

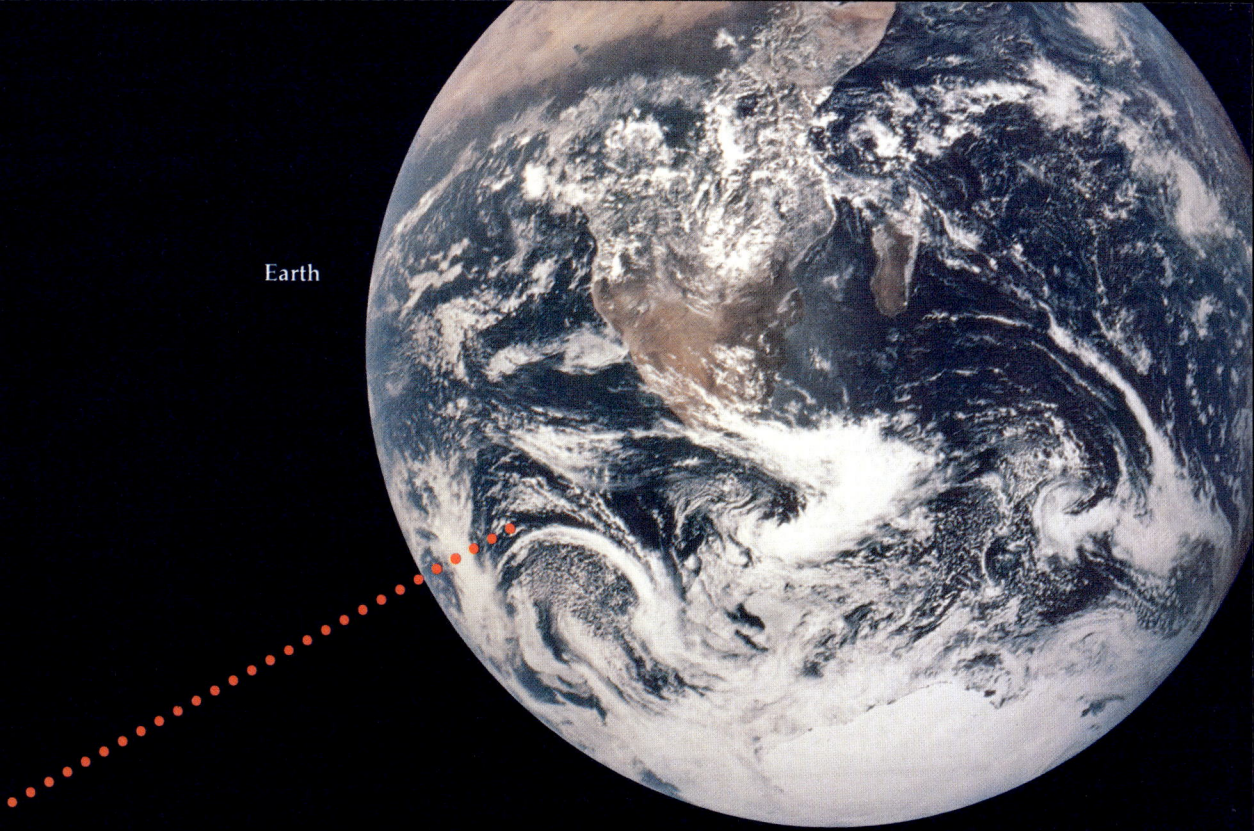

Earth

How it's done
The distance is equal to the speed of light multiplied by the time it takes to make the journey. As the beam goes to the Moon and back, the time must be halved to calculate the distance from Earth to Moon.

It takes four minutes for a particle of light (a photon) to make a *one-way* journey from the Sun to the Earth. How far away is the Earth from the Sun?

	equals		multiplied by	
Distance from Earth to Moon	**=**	Speed of light (299, 792 km per second)	**x**	One half the time the laser beam takes to reach the Moon and return

Planet time

How long is a day? On Earth it is about 24 hours. In fact the Earth is a poor timekeeper because it changes its speed with the movement of the tides, when Ice Ages come and go, with the orbit of the Moon and how close it comes to other planets. When we compare the way we measure time on Earth with that on other planets we find that neither an Earth day, nor an Earth year is very useful.

Sun
(yellow)

Mercury
a year is equal to 88 Earth days; a day is equal to 59 Earth days
(purple)

Venus
a year is equal to 225 Earth days; a day is equal to 243 Earth days
(green)

Earth
a year is equal to 365 Earth days; a day is 24 Earth hours
(blue)

Mars
a year is equal to 687 Earth days; a day is 24 Earth hours
(red)

Does the length of the Earth day change?

The Earth is slowing down. About five hundred million years ago the Earth took only 20 hours to spin once on its axis. Today it takes a little over 24 hours and in 200 million years time it will take 25 hours for the Earth to spin once on its axis.

Time on the planets

The length of a day is different on each planet in our **Solar System** because each planet spins at a different rate. The planet that spins fastest is Jupiter, at just under 10 hours, while the slowest is Mercury, which takes just under 59 days to spin once on its axis.

The length of a year also varies between planets, depending on how long it takes them to orbit the Sun.

A year on Pluto, one of the outer planets, will be 248 years if we measured it in Earth time. By contrast, Mercury orbits the Sun once every 88 Earth days.

(For more information on the Solar System see the books Falling (Gravity) *and* The Earth in Space *in the Science in our world series.)*

Jupiter
a year is equal to 12 Earth years; a day is equal to 10 Earth hours
(bands)

Saturn
a year is equal to 29 Earth years; a day is equal to 10 Earth hours
(rings)

Uranus
a year is equal to 84 Earth years; a day is equal to 23 Earth hours
(blue with rings)

Pluto
a year is equal to 248 Earth years; a day is equal to 6 Earth days
(grey)

Neptune
a year is equal to 164 Earth years; a day is equal to 22 Earth hours
(blue)

Light years and star time

Astronomers cannot use an ordinary clock on Earth as a timekeeper for the **Universe**. They need to use a constant timekeeper to measure the vast spaces between stars.

A constant timekeeper is the speed of light (see page 38). Astronomers use the *time* it takes for light to reach us to work out how *far* away each star or planet is. The basic unit for this is called a light year.

A light year
A light year is the distance light travels through space in one Earth year. This is the staggering distance of over 9 million million (9,460,000,000,000) km.

Using this system of measuring distances, Alpha Centauri, the nearest star to the Sun, is just over 4 light years away from us.

Each name on these maps represents a bright star

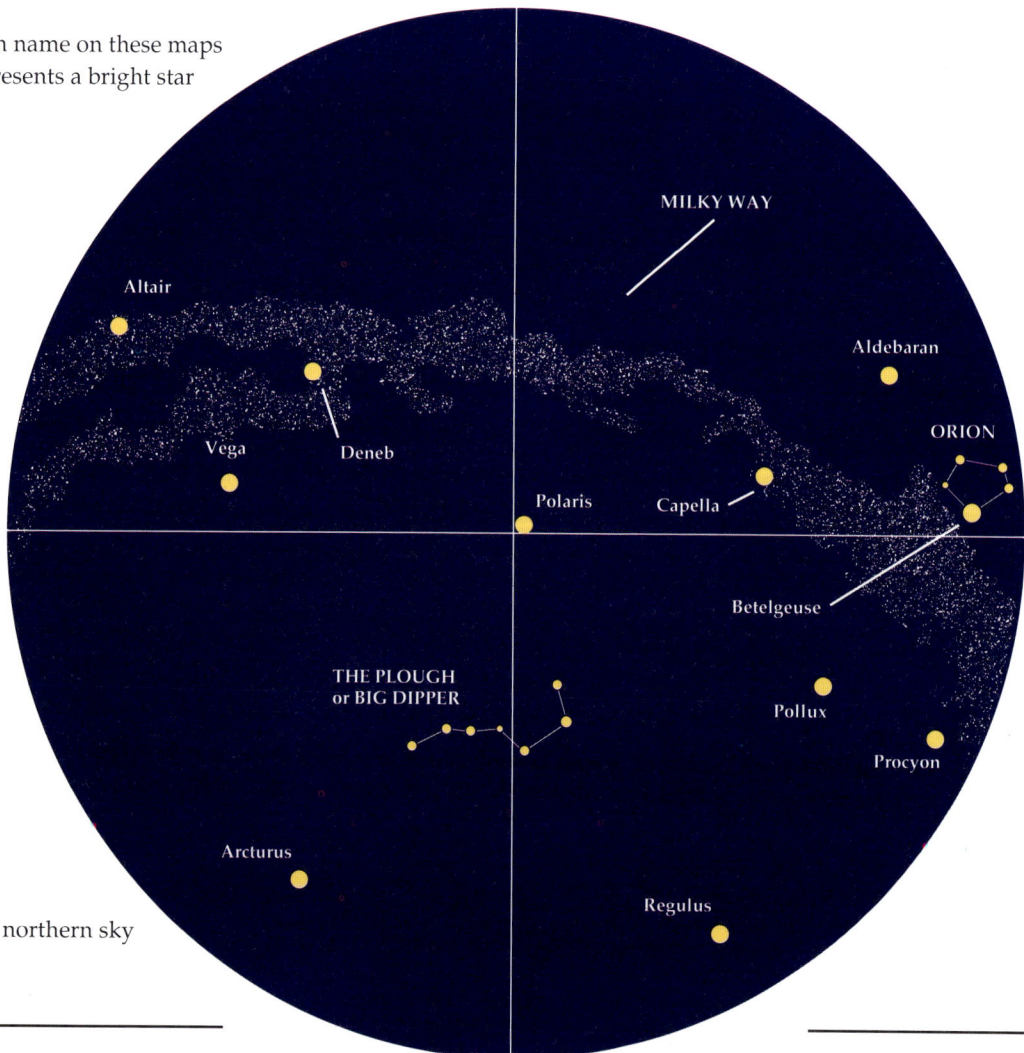

MILKY WAY

Altair

Aldebaran

ORION

Vega   Deneb

Polaris   Capella

Betelgeuse

THE PLOUGH
or BIG DIPPER

Pollux

Procyon

Arcturus

Regulus

The northern sky

Brightest stars	light years
Sirius	9
Canopus	181
Alpha centuri	4
Arcturus	36
Vega	26
Capella	46
Rigel	880
Procyon	11
Achernar	114
Beta centuri	423
Betelgeuse	586
Altair	16
Aldebaran	68
Alpha crucis	261
Antares	424
Spica	211
Pollux	35
Fomalhaut	23
Deneb	1630
Beta crucis	423
Regulus	85
Adhara	652

This table shows the brightest stars and their distance from Earth in light years

(For more information on planets, the Sun and stars see the book The Earth in Space *in the Science in our World series.)*

Light years see into the past

Light years are a kind of time machine. If you look at a star that is 200 light years away from us, you are seeing the light that came from that star 200 years ago.

This is the only way we can look into the past. But for the same reason we have no idea what is currently happening in the vastness of space because the light simply has not reached us yet!

The Milky Way, the galaxy of which our Solar System forms a tiny part, is shown here as a speckled band across both star maps. It is about 200,000 light years 'wide'.

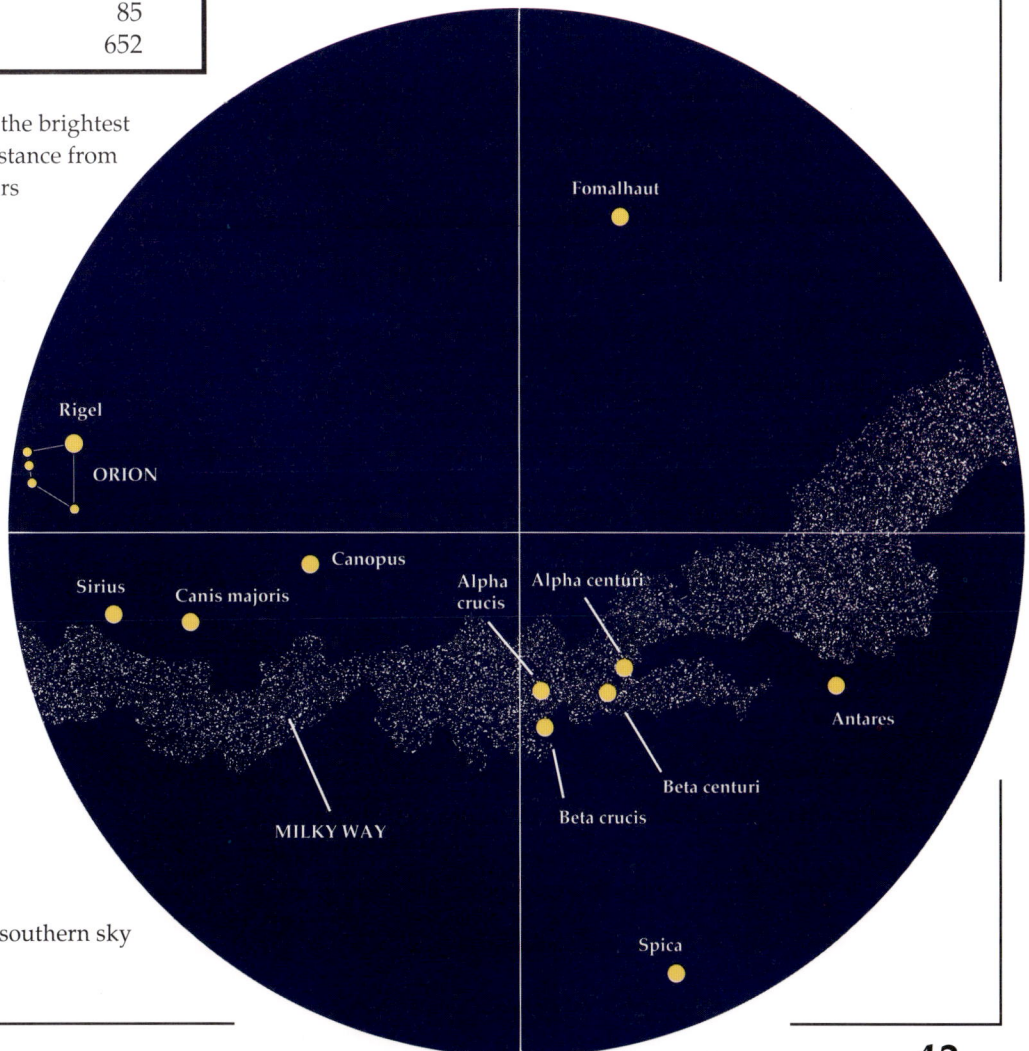

The southern sky

Fomalhaut

Rigel

ORION

Canopus

Sirius

Canis majoris

Alpha crucis

Alpha centuri

Antares

Beta centuri

Beta crucis

MILKY WAY

Spica

Time to form our Universe

We are used to measuring time in days and years, but our planet is over 4.6 billion years old.

Although it seems so old, the Earth is one of the youngest bodies in the Universe. The longest time we know of is the time since the start of our Universe. Unbelievable amounts of time have been needed to form all the stars and the planets, but scientists are now able to give us a glimpse back to the beginning and tell us how long it has taken.

The Big Bang

Scientists believe that all the stars and planets now in the Universe started out from a single very dense source. About 15 billion years ago a gigantic explosion occurred, throwing pieces out in all directions.

This 'first' event is called the Big Bang. As far as we can know, this is the start of time. Over the next thousands of millions of years, some of the pieces formed stars and planets. The rest still drifts as space dust.

15 billion years ago: The Big Bang

4.6 billion years ago:
the formation of the Earth

12 billion years
ago: galaxies form

The picture that fills
this page is a galaxy

Clues from meteorites

Meteoroids, or planetesimals, are small lumps of rock that drift about in space. It is believed that they have remained unchanged since the time when all the planets were formed.

Some meteoroids fall to the Earth and scientists can then find their age. They prove to be about 4.6 billion years old, showing that they formed at about the same time as the Earth, probably from a large spinning mass of rocks and dust.

A galaxy

A galaxy is a spinning collection of stars and planets. Seen from Earth, galaxies look like spinning discs. We now know that the main stars of the galaxies were formed about 12 billion years ago.

New words

arc
a small segment of a circle. A quarter of a circle has an arc of 90^0 for example

astronomy
the science of studying the Universe. Astronomers are concerned with the nature and origins of the Universe, including the Earth, but they do not study the Earth in detail

axis
an axis is the line around which a body spins. For example the axis around which a wheel spins is called the hub. All planets spin and so they can be thought of as having an axis through the line which is at the centre of the spin. The Earth's axis goes through the poles and it is at $23\frac{1}{2}^0$ to its orbit

chlorophyll
the green pigment in plant cells which can absorb the energy in sunshine and use it to help the plant create new tissue

co-ordinates
a system of describing the position of an object. The edge of a map, for example, is marked off in numbers which can then be used to describe the location of any feature. On the Earth the co-ordinates are longitude and latitude. A location might then be given as, for example, 45^0 W and 24^0 S (which is Sao Paulo in Brazil)

dimension
a basic unit that measures the Universe. The dimensions are length, mass and time

element
pure chemical substances (such as oxygen or iron) are called elements. Combinations of 105 elements make up the entire known Universe

equinox
a time when the length of the day and night are the same. An equinox happens when the Earth is at its shortest distance from the Sun, in March and September

Greenhouse Effect
the warming of the Earth's atmosphere as a result of pollution by carbon dioxide gas produced primarily by power stations and car exhausts

jet lag
people who make plane journeys have to wait for their biological clocks to adjust to local time – an effect travellers know as jet lag

lunar
anything that relates to the Moon. A lunar month is the time it takes for the Moon to change from new Moon through full Moon and back to new Moon again

mechanical
anything that relates to machines

microscopic

anything that is so small it can only be seen with the aid of a microscope. Usually objects smaller that a tenth of a millimetre need to be looked at with a microscope

migrate

the long distance movement that some animals make each year in order to find new sources of food. Migrations are most common in areas that experience strong seasonal problems, such as a summer drought or a harsh winter

pendulum

any object that can swing freely under the effects of gravity will make a pendulum. A pendulum has certain important properties including a regular time for each complete swing, known as the time period

period

the time it takes for a swinging body like a pendulum to complete one complete swing and return to its starting position

Solar System

the group of planets that is held in orbit by the gravitational attraction of the Sun

solstice

the time when the Earth is at its greatest distance from the Sun, in December and June each year

Index